W9-AKD-934

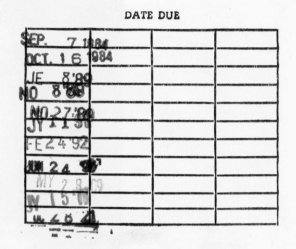

DATE DUE

SEP. 7 1984		
OCT. 16 1984		
JE 8 '89		
NO 8 89		
NO 27 '89		
JY 11 90		
FE 24 '92		
JN 24		
MY 28 '9		
JY 15 99		
JL 29		

J
920
Mu

**Mumford, Prudence
Famous names in crime**

EAU CLAIRE DISTRICT LIBRARY

FAMOUS NAMES
IN CRIME
PRUDENCE MUMFORD

81582

Wayland

EAU CLAIRE DISTRICT LIBRARY

5/27/83 Main Line 7 95

Other books in this series

Famous Names in Medicine
Famous Names in Space Exploration
Famous Names in Science
Famous Names in World Exploration
Famous Names in Music
Famous Names in Sport

ISBN 0 85340 635 9
© Copyright 1978 Wayland Publishers Ltd
First published in 1978 by
Wayland Publishers Limited,
49 Lansdowne Place, Hove,
East Sussex, BN3 1HF, England
Printed by Cahills, Dublin

CONTENTS

GUY FAWKES
and the gunpowder plot

Remember, remember the 5th of November, gunpowder, treason and plot! In the UK on 5th November each year there are bonfires and fireworks, to celebrate the death of Guy Fawkes. But what did he do?

Young Guy grew up in York in the 1570s. He had a stepfather who was Catholic—when most of the people who lived in England were Protestants. The king, James I, was Protestant and treated the Catholics very badly. So they wanted to kill him, and have a Catholic king. A group of important Catholic gentlemen made a daring plan to blow up the Houses of Parliament, while King James was there. They asked Guy Fawkes to help them.

They rented a house next door to the Houses of Parliament and Guy Fawkes went there as a servant. He called himself John Johnson. The plotters made the tunnel through to the Houses of Parliament. Meanwhile they had a stroke of luck. They managed to rent a cellar under the House of Lords!

This made their work much easier—they just had to put gunpowder in the cellar and light it when the king was in the House of Lords above. The whole building would blow up and the king would be killed!

Their amazing plot failed because one of them gave the rest away. At the last minute, the king's men had news of the Gunpowder Plot, as it was called. The explosion was fixed for 5th November. The night before, the king's soldiers crept down into the cellar. There was Guy Fawkes, guarding the gunpowder. The soldiers easily overpowered him, and dragged him off to the Tower of London. There he was tortured until he confessed all about the plot, and gave the names of the other plotters. They were all caught, and Guy Fawkes was executed as a traitor on 31st January, 1606.

CAPTAIN WILLIAM KIDD
piracy on the high seas

Piracy was particularly common after naval wars when crews were disbanded and pirate captains were able to offer them work of a different kind. Probably the most famous pirate in history was Captain Kidd. Kidd was a respectable sea captain until the age of fifty, and only went on one expedition as a pirate. What made him exceptional was the fact that he had been sent by the government to capture pirate ships at the time!

In 1695 the English Government was very worried about the effect of piracy on English trade abroad. Unfortunately England was at war with France and no naval ship could be spared. Therefore it was suggested that a privateer should be sent out against the pirates and Captain Kidd was appointed to command it. A privateer is a privately owned ship that is given permission by the Government to attack pirate or enemy ships. The crew of Kidd's ship, the *Adventure,* were to be paid in 'prize money' obtained by sale of the booty found on pirate ships. The *Adventure* sailed from Plymouth in May 1696 and, after stopping in New York to recruit seamen, set off for Madagascar, off the east coast of Africa, which was known as a hiding place of pirates. Once there, Kidd amazed his backers by turning into a pirate himself and attacking English and other friendly ships. His most valuable capture, the *Quedagh Merchant,* had a cargo worth £70,000 from the East. Soon after this, Kidd took two Armenian ships that he claimed were carrying French passes, which gave him the right to attack them. In April 1699 Kidd learnt that he had been declared a pirate. A squadron of ships was made ready to sail in pursuit of him and the American colonies were ordered to seize him if he landed. In order to protect his booty, Kidd hid most of it on Gardiner's Island, then sank the *Quedagh Merchant* and continued in a sloop to Boston. There he tried to bargain for

his freedom but was tricked into going ashore and sent back to England to stand trial. After an unfair trial, he was hanged at Execution Dock. The members of the Government who had earlier supported Kidd's expedition were greatly criticized in Parliament.

Two hundred years later the French passes of the Armenian ships were found, which showed that Kidd was not guilty of piracy, at least in the case of those ships. The buried treasure from the *Quedagh Merchant* has never been recovered.

DICK TURPIN
English highwayman

"Stand and deliver—Your money or your life!" These words once struck terror into the hearts of people on England's roads. Two hundred years ago any long journey was a dangerous business. There were no railways and people who could afford to use them used stagecoaches. The danger came from highwaymen who very often attacked these stagecoaches. They always attacked on the open road far from any town—so no one would come to the rescue. They usually carried pistols and wore masks. Since there were no police to catch them, they were able to make a good living by stealing money and jewels.

Dick Turpin was the most famous English highwayman. Legend tells us he rode a beautiful, intelligent mare called Black Bess. He was a fierce robber, and sometimes murdered people who refused to hand over their jewels and money. He lived in a cave in Epping Forest, Essex. All those who made a journey through Essex were terrified of him. Eventually a huge reward was offered for his capture. At this time he was attacking a stagecoach almost every night. Then, quite suddenly, he disappeared.

About a year later a man calling himself John Palmer was arrested and charged with stealing sheep and horses. This John Palmer was none other than Dick Turpin in disguise. He wrote to his brother to ask for his help in getting out of jail. Unfortunately Dick forgot to pay for the postage of the letter, and when his brother was asked to pay instead, he did not recognise Dick's writing, and refused. The letter was also seen by the village schoolmaster. He remembered the writing on the letter—it was the writing of a little boy he had once taught—and the boy's name was Dick Turpin! The schoolmaster rushed to York to claim the reward. Dick Turpin was at last brought to justice. He was sentenced to death and hanged on the Knavesmire, York, in 1739. Before the executioner could take the ladder from under his feet, Dick jumped off and died bravely in the tradition of the highwaymen.

On the left, Dick Turpin holds up a lone rider in Epping Forest, Essex. Turpin, and highwaymen like him, made journeys very dangerous before special mounted patrols were set up to protect road users.

THE MUTINY ON THE BOUNTY
tyranny and revenge at sea

HMS *Bounty* left Spithead on 23rd December, 1787, to carry a cargo of bread-fruit plants from Tahiti, in the South Pacific, to the British colonies in the West Indies. Captain Cook had discovered the fruit and the Navy Board had decided to grow it in the West Indies as food for the slaves on the plantations. The *Bounty* was a small ship of 215 tons and the 46 men aboard were very cramped. The captain, Lieutenant William Bligh, was a good sailor, but he had a terrible temper and behaved like a tyrant. The voyage out was long and hard—the *Bounty* did not reach Tahiti until 26th October, 1788. On the way there were fierce storms and, when rations became short, Bligh made the crew eat bad fruit.

The *Bounty* stayed nearly six months at Tahiti and the crew became idle in the tropical heat. When the ship sailed again on 4th April, 1789, Bligh found that the crew was unwilling to take orders. Bligh had a particular dislike for Fletcher Christian, the second-in-command, who was a sensitive person and in every way the opposite of Bligh. Finally, on 27th April, Bligh insulted Christian by calling him a coward and a thief for no reason. Christian decided to desert the ship. He was unable to get away that night unnoticed, so the next morning he decided to take over the ship. He knew this would be mutiny—a crime punishable by death. Before sunrise, with the help of nine crew members who also hated the captain, Christian overpowered the officers. He then forced Bligh and eighteen loyal men over the side into a small boat with a compass but no maps, and just enough food and water to survive. From there, facing exposure, hunger and thirst, and having to eat sea birds and shellfish to make their rations last, they sailed 5,800 kilometres across the Pacific Ocean. Miraculously, twelve out of the nineteen reached the island of

Timor, north of Australia, nearly three months later. From there, the survivors took a boat back to England, arriving in March 1790.

Meanwhile the twenty-five mutineers returned to Tahiti. Then nine of them, including Christian and John Adams, decided to found a colony with some of the native Polynesians on the remote Pitcairn Islands, where they would be unlikely to be found. The other sixteen stayed at Tahiti. In 1791 HMS *Pandora* arrived in search of them. They were captured and sent back to England for trial, and three of them executed. The Pitcairn colonists were not discovered until an American ship accidentally landed there in 1808. John Adams was the only mutineer still alive and he said Christian had been murdered many years before. No one knows the truth, as one of the crew claimed he had secretly made his way back to England quite soon after the mutiny and had even been seen in the streets of Devonport!

SIR ROBERT PEEL
and the police force

Imagine London with no policemen! More than a hundred years ago, when the cities were full of crime, there was no police force. The only crime-fighters then were a group of men called the Bow Street Runners.

They were plain-clothes detectives, who tried to track down criminals and bring them to trial. At first there were only six of them to cover the whole of London! They were paid nothing, but lived off rewards offered by the victims of crime.

At first the Runners did a good job in clearing the streets of robbers. But they were often dishonest, and accepted bribes. The job of dealing with crime was just too big for them. There were street riots at the time, and they could not keep order.

Sir Robert Peel was Home Secretary in 1829. He saw that London needed a well-organized police force. England was the only country in Europe without one. He took the advice of the magistrates Henry Fielding and Patrick Colquhoun. They persuaded Parliament to pass a law, setting up the Metropolitan Police Force. Sir Robert's police were to be

dressed in a dark blue uniform. Their job was to patrol the streets of London and deal with any crime committed in the capital. They first appeared in September 1829, and have been on patrol ever since.

These first policemen were nicknamed "Peelers" or "Bobbies" after their founder, Sir Robert Peel. At first they did not act as detectives, and the Bow Street Runners continued to be in charge of detecting criminals. But in 1842 a special Detective branch of the Metropolitan Police was formed. Peel's police force was a great success. It was a full-time, properly paid and trained organization. The "Peelers" caught criminals and prevented crime as well. Above all, they were independent and uncorrupt. Within thirty years police forces had been set up by towns and counties throughout the country.

13

EAU CLAIRE DISTRICT LIBRARY

JESSE JAMES
and his gang

Jesse James and his brother Frank were country boys, born on a farm in America. When they were young men the Civil War broke out. The Northern states of America fought the Southern states. Jesse and Frank were too young to join either army, but they had guns and they wanted to fight. They joined a gang, called the Quantrill gang. They fought the Northern soldiers, attacking them and laying ambushes. They used to hide in the woods and make surprise attacks on their enemies. This was good training for Jesse and Frank; they learned to hide, to attack, and to get away safely. When the war ended, their Southern side had lost. Jesse and Frank needed money, so they formed their own gang.

The James gang soon grew famous, living by robbing trains and banks. They became the most famous and fierce outlaws in the Wild West. Many sheriffs tried to catch them, but the brothers had learned clever escape-tricks. In 1874, lawmen took their revenge. They set fire to the house where Jesse and Frank's mother lived. Jesse and Frank escaped unhurt, but their little brother was killed and the house burned down.

At last, a reward of $5,000 was offered for Jesse James or his brother Frank—dead or alive! In 1882 Bob Ford joined their gang. He was secretly working for the sheriff, and wanted the reward. He shot Jesse in the back of the head as he was dusting a picture in his home. Although Jesse was an outlaw and had killed many people during his robberies, people thought Bob Ford was wrong to shoot Jesse James when he was unarmed and unprepared. Frank soon gave himself up to the sheriff, and Bob Ford got the $5,000 reward.

SIR BERNARD SPILSBURY
criminal pathologist

Pathology had been an unpopular and backward subject until
Sir Bernard Spilsbury brought it up to date and made it
respectable. A pathologist studies disease; he often helps the
police to investigate crimes involving a death. He performs a
post-mortem ("after-death") operation, or an autopsy, to find
out whether the cause of death was natural (like illness), an
accident, suicide, or an attack from an unknown criminal. He
decides how each injury was caused. He will try to estimate
when the person died, and look for unusual things, like scars,
to help the police identify the body. Finally, he may do special
tests, like finding out the blood group of the dead person, in
case blood is found on a knife or gun or on the clothes of a
suspect.

Sir Bernard Spilsbury's first great case was the trial of Dr
Crippen. Dr Crippen was accused of poisoning his wife. Police
found a body buried at Dr Crippen's house and cut up into
pieces. Sir Bernard found a scar on a piece of skin that was
the same as a scar known to have been on the stomach of Mrs
Crippen. Sir Bernard also detected traces of a drug on the
body, and it was known that Dr Crippen had bought enough of
this drug to kill someone, shortly before his wife disappeared.
Without this evidence Dr Crippen could not have been found
guilty.

For thirty years after this trial Spilsbury appeared at almost
every murder trial in the south of England. He often gave
evidence which convicted murderers, and was the perfect
scientific witness, always keeping calm under cross-
examination. In 1924 his evidence was again vital when he
put together the scattered remains of the murdered Emily
Kaye in the Mahon case. The next year he faced eight medical
experts for the defence who said that Elsie Cameron had
hanged herself and had not been murdered by Thorne.
Spilsbury thought it was murder and the jury believed him, not

the eight others! But Spilsbury sometimes appeared for the defence. In the Cornock case, he was sure that Mrs Cornock had not killed her husband. But he was not happy with the defence until he had enough evidence to convince the jury that Mr Cornock's injuries could not have been caused by his wife. The jury accepted his story and Mrs Cornock was found not guilty.

The science of pathology has become more complicated since Spilsbury's day. With modern scientific machines, the pathologist can help the detective obtain vital clues from a speck of dust, a hair, a tiny bloodstain or a chip of paint. The pathologist can look at the very atoms from which these things are made. He has swapped his magnifying glass for complicated equipment like the mass spectrometer, the laser beam, the computer, and even the atomic reactor.

WYATT EARP
sheriff of the wild west

If you like Western movies and cowboy stories you will have heard of Wyatt Earp. He was one of the most famous sheriffs of the Wild West. He had two brothers, Morgan and Virgil, and all three of them were determined to bring law and order to the towns where they lived. It was a time of outlaws, thieves, horse stealers, cattle rustlers and murderers. There were famous bad men too—Jesse James, John Wesley Hardin and Wild Bill Hickok. They stole and murdered without fear of the law because no sheriff had enough men or guns to stop them.

In 1879, Wyatt Earp became marshal of Tombstone, Arizona. He and his brothers wanted to make life safe for ordinary people in Tombstone. They had to arrest Old Man Clanton, the McLowery brothers, and their gang, who were terrorizing the town with their shooting raids. In 1881 the Clantons' gang told Wyatt Earp that he must leave Tombstone or die. Wyatt Earp was not afraid. He dared the gang to try and kill him. The two sides met in a pitched battle at the OK Corral. On Wyatt Earp's side were his brothers Virgil and Morgan, and their friend Doc Holliday. Against them stood Ike and Billy Clanton, two sons of Old Man Clanton, Frank and Tom McLowery, and Billy Claiborne. The gunfight lasted between 15 and 30 seconds, and 34 shots were fired. The two McLowery brothers and Billy Clanton were killed. Morgan and Virgil Earp were slightly wounded. But Wyatt Earp and Doc Holliday were unhurt; the rest of the Clanton gang ran away, and Tombstone was rid of its outlaw gang.

Wyatt Earp lived until long after the Wild West was finally tamed. He died peacefully in 1929, aged 80, and he is still remembered today as the most famous sheriff in the West.

The picture on the right shows Wyatt Earp in 1885.

19

JACK THE RIPPER
the terror of London

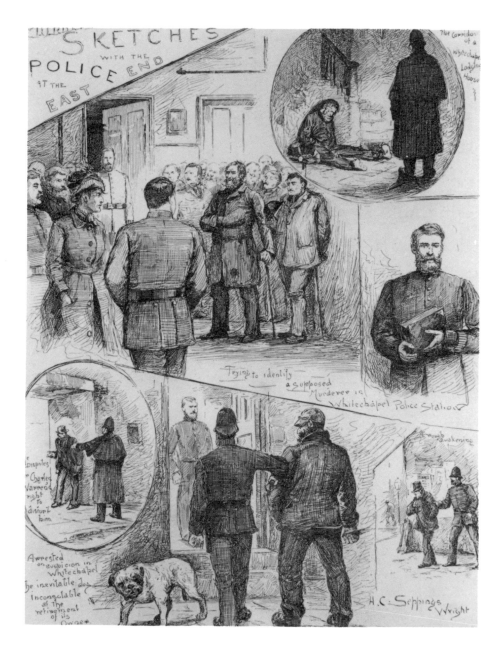

Jack the Ripper is the name given to one of the most horrible murderers in history. He was never caught. His nickname came from the letters that he wrote to the police which he signed, "Yours truly, Jack the Ripper". All the murders happened in a very small area of the East End of London, around Whitechapel. This is why they are sometimes called the Whitechapel murders. All the women killed were prostitutes who lived alone and were often out on the streets. On 6th August, 1888, Martha Turner was murdered in Whitechapel. Her throat was slit by a knife with a long blade. From then until the end of that year the people in the East End lived in terror of the Ripper. The next five murders were even more gruesome. The Ripper first slit the victim's throat, and then mutilated the body. The last murder, on 9th November, was the most ghastly. Mary Kelly was stabbed with a knife, her throat was cut, and the Ripper cut out her heart and kidneys, and laid them on a table. Bits of the body were laid in little heaps around the room.

Many people were suspected, but the police could never prove that any of them was the murderer. One great clue was that the murderer knew something about surgical operations. The bodies were very neatly cut up. Was the Ripper a doctor? There was one main suspect, called Vassily Konovalov. (He called himself many other names to hide from the police.) He was a Russian, who helped a doctor at a London clinic. Police think he treated some of the women who became the Ripper's victims. Konovalov was thought to have killed and cut up a woman in Paris before he came to London, and later in Russia he murdered again. Only one man ever saw the Ripper closely, and he said Konovalov looked very like him. But Konovalov left London and went back to Russia so he was never caught.

We shall never know who was the real Jack the Ripper.

The sketches on the left show the police busy investigating the Ripper murders. The police came under criticism for their failure to find the murderer. It was even suggested that the authorities knew who the Ripper was, but because he was an important man they would not arrest him. Modern investigation suggests there may be some truth in this idea.

SIR EDWARD HENRY
and the use of fingerprints

Sir Edward Henry was not the first person to think of using fingerprints in hunting criminals, but it was he who made the idea work. Sir William Herschel showed that the fingerprints of a person never change. Then Francis Galton worked out that no two people have the same fingerprints.

Sir Edward first became interested in fingerprints when he was an inspector of police in India. Fingerprints were often used as a kind of signature by people who could not write. This made Henry think they could help in tracking down criminals. He worked out a system of classifying fingerprints that left almost no room for mistakes and made it possible to look up a set of fingerprints very quickly. In 1897 he persuaded the Indian police to use his system and four years later the British police started to use it as well. In its first year the Central Fingerprint Bureau helped the police identify four times as many criminals as before. The use of fingerprints to solve the Deptford "masked" murder case convinced the public of their value.

ARCHES   LOOPS   WHORLS

In 1901 Henry returned to England to become Head of the Criminal Investigation Department (C.I.D.) of the Metropolitan Police. His job was to set up fingerprint records at Scotland Yard. There are now well over $1\frac{1}{2}$ million sets of fingerprints, with each set made up of the fingers and thumbs of both hands. There are also a lot of odd prints taken from the scenes of unsolved crimes, which can then be matched with suspects' prints later.

DR CRIPPEN
a murderer caught by wireless telegram

Dr Crippen was a short, quiet man who came from Michigan, USA in 1900 to live in London. He was married to an untidy, noisy woman called Cora. They lived at 39 Hilldrop Crescent in Camden Town, London. Dr Crippen worked as a manager of a medicine business. In the office he met and fell in love with a quiet, shy girl called Ethel Le Neve.

The picture shows Mrs Crippen, when she was a singer.

25

To all their friends Dr and Mrs Crippen seemed a happy pair, but underneath he grew to hate his wife. In January 1910, Dr Crippen ordered some hyoscine, a poisonous drug. On 31st January they had some friends to supper. That evening was the last time Mrs Crippen was ever seen alive.

Soon Ethel Le Neve moved in with Dr Crippen. A woman in the street suspected that the doctor had murdered his wife, and went to Scotland Yard. Chief Inspector Dew and Sergeant Mitchell went to see Dr Crippen. He said his wife had left him and gone back to America. Chief Inspector Dew sent out a description of Mrs Crippen. He went back to visit Dr Crippen at his office—but he was not there. Nor was he at home. Inspector Dew looked around, and started a thorough search which took three days. At last, on 13th July, the police found traces of a dead body in the coal cellar. It was the body of Mrs Crippen. It had been cut up into small pieces. All the bones had been removed from it.

On 16th July, the police went to arrest Dr Crippen, but he and Ethel Le Neve were already on board the SS *Montrose* on their way to Canada. Ethel was dressed up as a boy, but the captain of the ship saw them holding hands and guessed who they were. He sent a telegram to Scotland Yard on 22nd July by the ship's wireless. It was the first time a wireless telegram had been used in a criminal case. The next day Dew and Mitchell boarded the *Montrose* and arrested them. Back in London, Dr Crippen was tried and convicted of the murder of his wife and hanged on 23rd November, 1910. The court did not think Ethel Le Neve knew about her lover's wickedness, so they let her go and she went to live in America.

THE LINDBERGH KIDNAPPING

In 1927 Colonel Charles Lindbergh became the first man ever to fly across the Atlantic Ocean non-stop from New York to Paris. It took him $33\frac{1}{2}$ hours alone in his monoplane and his adventure made him a hero in both countries. So everyone was horrified to hear that his baby son had been kidnapped.

It happened in March 1932. Both Colonel and Mrs Lindbergh were at home in New Jersey, USA when the baby Charles was kidnapped from his nursery between eight and ten o'clock at night. His nurse, Betty Gow, discovered that he was missing. The New Jersey police were told immediately. They discovered that the kidnapper had used a long folding ladder to get into the nursery window and they found some footprints under the window. They also found a ransom note for $50,000 (equal to about £10,000 at the time). This meant that whoever had taken baby Charles would only let him go if Colonel and Mrs Lindbergh paid them that amount of money. But who should they pay? No one knew who could have taken the baby. No one had seen the kidnapping. No one had any clue. Five days later the Lindberghs got another ransom note. This time more money was demanded. The next day they got yet another note demanding nearly $70,000. By this time the public were very worried and upset. A doctor called John Condon offered to act as a go-between and to take the money from Lindbergh to the kidnappers. The kidnappers sent a note to the doctor to say that this was a good idea. They arranged to meet.

On 13th March, Dr Condon went to the meeting place, Woodlawn Cemetery in New York City, where he met a man who called himself John, who said the baby was alive and well. As a sign of this Dr Condon was sent some baby's clothes which were identified by the parents. In April another meeting was arranged. Dr Condon took the money and met

John at the cemetery. John collected the money and told Dr Condon the baby was on a boat in Massachusetts. The police immediately went there, but found no baby. It had all been a heartless trick, and the cruel joker had got away with all the money.

Eventually, on 12th May, the dead body of baby Charles was found 8 kilometres from his parents' home. The coroner said he had been dead for about two months. He had been killed by a knock on the head. The FBI took up the search. They were now looking for a kidnapper and a murderer. At last, by carefully studying the handwriting of the ransom notes, and by tracing the money paid out by Dr Condon, the FBI tracked down Bruno Richard Hauptmann. They arrested him and he was tried for the murder of Charles Lindbergh Junior. In his flat police found more ransom notes. Samples of his handwriting showed that he had written all the ransom notes. Hauptmann was found guilty of the murder and was electrocuted on 3rd April, 1936.

J EDGAR HOOVER
Director of the FBI

At only twenty-nine, J Edgar Hoover became Director of the Bureau of Investigation. At that time most policemen worked for local police forces, which had no close links with one another. America is so vast that criminals could escape arrest by moving from one police area to another. Hoover had a huge job. He had to change a corrupt and inefficient Bureau into the main force against serious crime. He picked only the cleverest and fittest men as his special agents. His G-men (a nickname that meant "Government-men") went to a special school to be trained in the use of guns, self-defence and scientific detection. He increased the number of agents from about 650 to 7,000. He gave the National Crime Laboratory the job of forensic science and keeping records of fingerprints, photographs and details of appearance. Any police force looking for a criminal could use the Laboratory records and trace any known criminal quickly.

The crime wave and gang warfare in the 1930s forced the Government to give the re-named Federal Bureau of Investigation power to investigate all major crime. By 1935 it was clear the FBI was winning the battle.

During World War II, FBI agents arrested 16,000 Germans and Japanese. 1,700 were seized within twenty-four hours of the outbreak of the war in America.

After the war, the FBI led the fight against communism. FBI agents worked under cover to find out the names of the communist leaders. The FBI also found out who had betrayed atomic bomb secrets to the Russians. An Englishman was sent to prison for fourteen years and an American couple were executed for treason.

America's "top cop" served eight Presidents during his forty years as head of the FBI. One president called him "the hero of millions of honest citizens and the terror of all criminals".

PHILBY, BURGESS AND MACLEAN modern spies

Kim Philby, Guy Burgess (below) and Donald Maclean (above) were probably the most successful modern spies. All three men came from similar well-to-do families. They had been friends together at Cambridge University in the early 1930s and like many students became interested in communism. They decided to put their ideas into practice, and agreed to work as spies for the Russians.

In 1940 Philby was offered a job by the Secret Intelligence Service, or SIS. The SIS, also called MI6, is in charge of

ordinary intelligence work and counter-intelligence work against foreign spies abroad. MI5 deals with counter-intelligence work inside Britain. Philby was popular and very good at his job, so it was no surprise when he was made head of a new intelligence department formed to spy on Russia, which was then still an ally of Britain against Germany. Burgess also provided information for the Russians, first as a member of SIS, then of the Foreign Office, where he joined Maclean who had been there since 1935. But it was after the war, while working in America, that the three, particularly Philby, did the most damage. Maclean had been sent to Washington in 1944 and three years later he became British secretary of a joint British, American and Canadian committee dealing with atomic energy. At the time the Americans knew how to make an atomic bomb, but the Russians did not. For eighteen months Maclean gave Russia vital details of the military plans of Britain and America. Soon after Maclean left Washington to go to another job, Philby arrived. His job was to take charge of information passed between SIS and its new American equivalent, the CIA. The CIA was so impressed by the war record of the SIS that Philby was told everything he wanted to know about American secrets. And everything he was told was passed straight to the Russians. So it was not surprising that American plans misfired, like the Albanian uprising against the communists which never got started.

By 1950 it was obvious that a spy had been at work in Washington and Philby heard that Maclean was suspected. He told Burgess to warn Maclean and the two of them fled immediately abroad and then to Russia on 25th May, 1951, the very day the Foreign Secretary gave orders for Maclean to be interrogated. Because of his link with both men and the fact that he knew that Maclean was suspected, Philby was thought to be the "third man" who had warned them, but no-one could prove it. Five years later he began to work for SIS again, this time in the Middle East, until in 1961 a Russian spy came to the West and admitted that Philby was also one. Then, in 1963, Philby too disappeared and was next seen in Moscow. So, the three spies were finally uncovered, but only after countless secrets had been disclosed.

AL CAPONE
the Chicago gangster

Al Capone's family were very poor Italians living in the slums of New York City. Al Capone left school when he was only ten or eleven to make money for the family. He didn't earn money so much as steal it! He grew to be a big, strong, fierce-looking boy, with a scar from a fight wound down his left cheek. Everyone called him Scarface.

In 1920 a gangster called Big Jim Colosimo brought him to Chicago. Al became head of his own huge, fierce gang of thieves, murderers and bootleggers. The Prohibition Bill made it illegal to buy, sell, or drink alcohol. Al Capone's gang sold drink and protected the drinkers from the police. They carried sawn-off shotguns, and would shoot policemen and other gangsters who tried to stop them. They became very rich.

Gangster wars between Al Capone's men and others went on all through the 1920s. The worst murder was called The St Valentine's Day Massacre, because it happened on 14th February, 1929. Seven men from a rival gang were put against a wall and machine-gunned down in cold blood by Capone's men.

Al Capone broke the law openly. But he was not arrested by the police, nor killed by other gangs. He was so powerful and rich that he bribed the police and his accusers so he stayed free. At last, in 1931, Al Capone was sent to prison for eleven years. Not for murder, nor for bootlegging, but for failing to pay income tax! Capone said he did not know he had to pay tax on illegal income.

Al Capone was let out early for good conduct. By then he was an ill man, and went to live quietly in Florida. He died in 1947 of a heart attack. World War II had just ended, and so many people had died that Al Capone's death was hardly noticed.

CHRISTIE AND EVANS
of 10 Rillington Place

Number 10 Rillington Place looked a very ordinary house from the outside. But inside, the police found the remains of no less than seven murdered women. The question is, were they the victims of one murderer or two?

John Christie lived with his wife in the ground floor flat at 10 Rillington Place, Kensington, London. In 1948, young Timothy Evans, his wife Beryl and baby daughter Geraldine came to live in the top floor flat above the Christies. Mr and Mrs Evans were not happy together. They often quarrelled about money, and were seen fighting. In 1949 Evans suddenly left the flat and went to live with his aunt in Wales, without his wife or his baby. The police were alerted by Mrs Evans' father, who had last seen his daughter on 5th November, 1949. They searched the house and, to their horror, found the bodies of Mrs Evans and the baby in the wash-house. Evans had given himself up to the police, confessing not to murder, but to failing to report his wife's accidental death. He later confessed to strangling them both, was tried, found guilty and hanged at Pentonville prison on 9th March, 1950.

The Christies continued to live at Rillington Place, but some time in December 1950 Mrs Christie disappeared. Her husband gave several reasons for her absence. But in March 1952 he suddenly left the flat and took all his things with him. Another tenant moved in.

One day he was putting up a shelf in the kitchen when he discovered an opening in the wall. Tearing off the wallpaper he looked inside and found the bodies of three women. But not one of them was Mrs Christie! When the police searched the house, they found the body of Mrs Christie under the floorboards and two skeletons buried in the garden. The skeletons were those of women murdered eight years before. The three bodies were women murdered very recently. On 31st March, 1953 Christie was arrested on the bank of the Thames at Putney.

At his trial, Christie admitted strangling all six women. But, more terrible than this, he also confessed to murdering Mrs Evans. This shocked everyone—perhaps Evans was innocent, and had been wrongly hanged? It was Christie's story that had convinced the court that Evans was guilty. He now said that he had lied. People now remembered that Evans had accused Christie of murdering his baby, but no one had believed him. It also seemed unlikely that two murderers, both stranglers, should have been living in the same house at the same time. Christie was found guilty, sentenced to death, and hanged.

Because of public pressure, there were two inquiries set up to see whether Evans was innocent. In the more recent of these, in 1965, the evidence showed that Evans might not have been guilty. In 1966 the Queen granted him a free pardon, 16 years after his death.

THE KRAY TWINS
London gangsters

Ronnie and Reggie Kray were identical twins born in the East End of London in 1934. In the East End violence and strength meant power. The twins grew into the strongest and most violent boys in the area. They began the protection racket that made and kept them rich for nearly fifteen years.

The Krays' gang was known as The Firm throughout the East End. It was the biggest and roughest gang and no one threatened The Firm. Anyone who opposed them would be knifed or very badly beaten up. George Cornell belonged to a rival gang, the Richardsons, and indirectly threatened the Krays. Ronnie Kray shot him through the head as he sat drinking in a Bethnal Green pub, The Blind Beggar.

Ronnie liked to think he was an English Al Capone. The Firm soon became involved in larger businesses than the protection racket. They dealt in fraud, and gambling, and tried to arrange a meeting with the American Mafia so that they could expand their illegal business activities. Meanwhile, Ronnie horribly knifed and murdered one of their old allies, Jack "the Hat" McVitie, because he had boasted that he was not afraid of the Krays.

A wall of fear stopped any of the Krays' enemies giving evidence in a case against them. At Scotland Yard, Inspector "Nipper" Read was in charge of the investigations, and for nearly a year a special department worked under cover to amass evidence. On 9th May, 1968, in a series of dawn raids, twenty-four of The Firm and the twins themselves were arrested. All the members of The Firm were safely in jail. More information then came to the police and the twins were charged with the murders of Cornell and McVitie.

At the Old Bailey on 8th March, 1969, the twins were found guilty, and sentenced to life imprisonment. They are still serving that sentence in Parkhurst Prison, Isle of Wight.

THE ASSASSINATION OF PRESIDENT KENNEDY
22nd November, 1963

It was a mild November day. The streets of Dallas, in Texas, USA, were full of excited people waiting to see the President pass by on his way to a civic lunch in the city centre. President Kennedy was popular with the American people. Families had been waiting for hours for the procession from the airport. President Kennedy and his wife were in an open car so that everyone would be able to see them clearly. They were smiling and waving to the crowd when suddenly a shot rang out, then another and another. The President slumped into his wife's arms, shot through the head and neck. Secret servicemen leapt onto the car to try to protect him, but the fatal shot had already been fired. The car rushed to the local hospital, but within thirty-five minutes of the shooting the President was dead.

Secret servicemen and police quickly discovered that the shots had come from the Texas Schoolbook Depository. A man in the crowd had seen a rifle pointing from an upper window. A policeman also heard the shot and rushed into the building. On the second floor he stopped a man who was walking through the canteen. But the caretaker knew him as he worked there, and they did not suspect him. His name was Lee Harvey Oswald. Inside the building the rifle was found and was soon identified as belonging to Oswald. A description of Oswald was given out on the radio to all policemen. Minutes later Oswald was stopped by a police patrolman. He pulled out a revolver and shot the policeman four times, then ran into a nearby cinema to hide. He was seen, followed and arrested, and charged with two murders: those of the police patrolman and the President of the United States. But Oswald never stood trial. The next day he too was killed. Jack Ruby, a night club owner who said he was horrified by the death of President Kennedy, shot Oswald from point-blank range, as he was taken from police headquarters to the county jail. Ruby was seen shooting Oswald by millions of viewers watching the television news (above). He was arrested for murder, tried, and sentenced to death.

THE GREAT TRAIN ROBBERY
8th August, 1963

It was a quarter past three in the morning. The mail train was rushing through the Buckinghamshire countryside on its way to Euston station, London. On the train postmen were sorting the mail from Scotland. There was also a great deal of money. Suddenly the driver saw a red signal ahead, meaning that the train should stop. This was not unusual. He ground to a halt. The co-driver got down from the train to see what was causing the delay, when suddenly he was grabbed by two men and taken back to the engine. There he saw that the driver had been overpowered, and that nine or ten more masked men were on the train. The train was being robbed!

The gang quickly uncoupled the engine and the first carriage, which carried the money, from the rest of the train. The driver was ordered to drive these two coaches up the track to a bridge. On the road under the bridge a truck and two Land Rovers were waiting. They used a pick-axe to open the carriage containing the money and quickly handcuffed the four postmen who were guarding the money inside. Then they threw the money bags over the bridge. More members of the gang caught the sacks and quickly stacked them in the Land Rovers. In less than fifteen minutes the gang had stolen more than two and a half million pounds! The back part of the train was left down the track. It was not until the guard got out to see why they were still sitting there, that the robbery was discovered. He saw that the engine was missing, and ran to Cheddington, the nearest station, to sound the alarm!

Next day the hunt was on! It was the biggest and most daring robbery of all time. The police had one clue: someone had seen the getaway truck rushing through the countryside after the robbery, and had told the police. The police were sure they were hiding not far away. Five days later they found the hideout. The farm was Leatherslade Farm, near Brill in Buckinghamshire. The robbers had gone, but had left mailbags, fingerprints and other clues behind them.

One by one, the gang was arrested. The fingerprints they had left proved they had been in the robbery. Most of the two and a half million pounds has never been recovered. The robbers who were found guilty were sentenced to thirty years in prison each. The most famous of the train robbers is Ronald Biggs. He escaped from prison in July 1965 by jumping over the wall of Wandsworth Jail onto the roof of a specially-built van, which was waiting ready for him. He has never been brought back to prison, and lives free in Brazil, South America.

Above left, Scotland Yard detectives at the scene of the crime. Below, Ronald Biggs in Rio de Janeiro, Brazil.

THE WATERGATE AFFAIR
downfall of a President

In November 1972 the Republican Richard Nixon was re-elected President of the United States with a great majority over his opponent from the Democratic party. Yet less than two years later he had been forced to resign in disgrace.

It all began with a burglary (called a "break-in" by Americans) on 17th June, 1972 at the skyscraper Watergate building in Washington, which was being used by Nixon's opponents, the Democrats, as their election headquarters. The burglars were caught in the act and put on trial. At first no one thought it important amid the excitement of an election. The *Washington Post* newspaper sent only two junior reporters, Bob Woodward and Carl Bernstein, to report the trial. But they discovered three things: the burglars had been trying to "bug"

the Democratic offices; one of the burglars, James McCord, had worked for the Government and for the Republican party; and, most important, McCord's address book contained the name of Howard Hunt, who had worked for Nixon in the White House. The two reporters became convinced that the burglary had been done on the orders of the Republican party and perhaps of Nixon himself. But nobody believed them.

They followed up every clue that might support their case and talked to hundreds of active Republicans. Then, in March 1973, McCord admitted that there were others involved in the burglary. At last Americans began to believe what Woodward and Bernstein had been saying. The Senate had meanwhile set up a committee to investigate the affair.

At first Nixon refused to allow his staff to appear as witnesses, then when he changed his mind, three of them, including the top Government lawyer, resigned. In May 1973 Nixon's legal adviser, John Dean, amazed the committee by saying that Nixon knew about the burglary beforehand and had agreed to pardon the burglars and pay them to keep quiet. Another witness surprised everyone by saying that Nixon had tape-recorded all talks he had had at the White House. Not surprisingly, the President refused to give up these tapes and when a judge demanded them, he was dismissed. This made the new top Government lawyer resign in protest and caused a great public outcry which made Nixon change his mind. For the second time in history, the House of Representatives began to consider impeaching a President. Although he had agreed to give up the tapes, Nixon spent the next seven months putting off doing so until the top court in the country ordered him to hand over all sixty-four tapes. It was now easy to see why he had not wanted anyone to hear them. They proved he had lied when he claimed he knew nothing about the burglary and in fact knew his staff were involved in it within a few days of its happening. They also showed he himself ordered his staff to cover up these facts. Soon his impeachment was recommended, but before this could happen, he resigned, on 9th August, 1974. No one doubted that it was only the hard work of the two reporters, Woodward and Bernstein, that had brought the whole affair to light.

Glossary

Autopsy   An operation to find out the cause of death.

Bootlegger   A supplier of illegal liquor.

Coroner   An official who at an inquest discovers how people have died.

Counter-Intelligence   Working against the enemy's spy system.

Execution Dock   A gallows for hanging pirates set by the River Thames to warn sailors.

Forensic Medicine   A branch of medicine concerned with the detection of crime.

Gallows   A wooden frame with a rope used to hang criminals.

House of Representatives   One of the Houses in the American parliament.

Intelligence (as used in spying)   Gathering information about the enemy.

Mutiny   Revolt against commanders in the army or navy.

Pathology   The study of disease and death.

Prohibition Bill   Name given to the Volstead Act of 17th January, 1920, in the USA which forbade the selling of alcohol.

Protection racket   An illegal way of forcing money from people in return for "protection" from violence.

Sloop   A small warship.

Treason   The crime of disloyalty to one's country.